Congratulations!

WELCOME TO THE REAL WORLD!

This is where the real "fun" begins!

Date: /   /

think positive

_____
_____
_____
_____
_____
_____
_____
_____
_____
_____
_____
_____
_____
_____
_____
_____
_____
_____
_____
_____
_____

THINGS TO BE GRATEFUL FOR TODAY

make it happen

Date: /   /

_____
_____
_____
_____
_____
_____
_____
_____
_____
_____
_____
_____
_____
_____
_____
_____
_____
_____

THINGS TO BE GRATEFUL FOR TODAY

> *"Miracles happen everyday, change your perception of what a miracle is and you'll see them all around you."* - Jon Bon Jovi

think positive

Date: /   /

_____
_____
_____
_____
_____
_____
_____
_____
_____
_____
_____
_____
_____
_____
_____
_____
_____
_____

THINGS TO BE GRATEFUL FOR TODAY

> *"If your dreams do not scare you, they are not big enough." - Ellen Johnson Sirleaf*

make it happen

Date: /   /

THINGS TO BE GRATEFUL FOR TODAY

think positive

Date: /   /

_____

_____

_____

_____

_____

_____

_____

_____

_____

_____

_____

_____

_____

_____

_____

_____

_____

THINGS TO BE GRATEFUL FOR TODAY

*make
it
happen*

Date: /   /

THINGS TO BE GRATEFUL FOR TODAY

"The only thing worse than starting something and failing... is not starting something." - Seth Godin

Date: /   /

think positive

_____
_____
_____
_____
_____
_____
_____
_____
_____
_____
_____
_____
_____
_____
_____
_____
_____
_____
_____

THINGS TO BE GRATEFUL FOR TODAY

make it happen

Date: /   /

THINGS TO BE GRATEFUL FOR TODAY

Date: /   /

think
positive

THINGS TO BE GRATEFUL FOR TODAY

"If you don't build your dream someone will hire you to help build theirs." — Tony Gaskins

make it happen

Date: / /

THINGS TO BE GRATEFUL FOR TODAY

think positive

Date: /   /

_____

_____

_____

_____

_____

_____

_____

_____

_____

_____

_____

_____

_____

_____

_____

_____

_____

_____

THINGS TO BE GRATEFUL FOR TODAY

> *"Never give up, for that is just the place and time that the tide will turn."* — Harriet Beecher Stow

make it happen

Date: ___ / ___ / ___

_____

_____

_____

_____

_____

_____

_____

_____

_____

_____

_____

_____

_____

_____

_____

_____

THINGS TO BE GRATEFUL FOR TODAY

think positive

Date: /   /

THINGS TO BE GRATEFUL FOR TODAY

> *"You just can't beat the person who never gives up."* — *Babe Ruth*

Date: /   /   *Take Action!*

_____

_____

_____

_____

_____

_____

_____

_____

_____

_____

_____

_____

_____

_____

_____

_____

THINGS TO BE GRATEFUL FOR TODAY

Date: /   /

think positive

THINGS TO BE GRATEFUL FOR TODAY

"Change your life today. Don't gamble on the future, act now, without delay." — Simone de Beauvoir

Date: /   /

Take Action!

_____
_____
_____
_____
_____
_____
_____
_____
_____
_____
_____
_____
_____
_____
_____
_____
_____
_____

THINGS TO BE GRATEFUL FOR TODAY

Date: /   /

think positive

THINGS TO BE GRATEFUL FOR TODAY

Date: /   /

Take Action!

THINGS TO BE GRATEFUL FOR TODAY

"Life is 10% what happens to you and 90% how you react to it." - Charles R. Swindoll

think positive

Date: /   /

THINGS TO BE GRATEFUL FOR TODAY

Date: /   /   Take Action!

_____

_____

_____

_____

_____

_____

_____

_____

_____

_____

_____

_____

_____

_____

_____

_____

_____

THINGS TO BE GRATEFUL FOR TODAY

"We may encounter many defeats but we must not be defeated." - Maya Angelou

think positive

Date: /   /

THINGS TO BE GRATEFUL FOR TODAY

Date: /   /   *Take Action!*

THINGS TO BE GRATEFUL FOR TODAY

"Opportunity does not knock, it presents itself when you beat down the door." - Kyle Chandler

think positive

Date: /   /

_____

_____

_____

_____

_____

_____

_____

_____

_____

_____

_____

_____

_____

_____

_____

_____

_____

_____

THINGS TO BE GRATEFUL FOR TODAY

Date: /   /   Take Action!

THINGS TO BE GRATEFUL FOR TODAY

Date: /   /

think positive

THINGS TO BE GRATEFUL FOR TODAY

make it happen

Date: /   /

THINGS TO BE GRATEFUL FOR TODAY

"Every accomplishment starts with the decision to try." - Brian Littrell

never ever give up

Date: /   /

_____
_____
_____
_____
_____
_____
_____
_____
_____
_____
_____
_____
_____
_____
_____
_____
_____
_____
_____
_____
_____
_____

THINGS TO BE GRATEFUL FOR TODAY

"Every great dream begins with a dreamer. Always remember, you have within you the strength, the patience, and the passion to reach for the stars to change the world." - Harriet Tubman

Take Action!

Date: /   /

THINGS TO BE GRATEFUL FOR TODAY

Date: /   /

never ever give up

THINGS TO BE GRATEFUL FOR TODAY

> *"It takes a strong person to do their own thing and not wait for anybody else to validate their existence." -*
> *Steven Aitchison*

think positive

Date: /   /

_____

_____

_____

_____

_____

_____

_____

_____

_____

_____

_____

_____

_____

_____

_____

_____

THINGS TO BE GRATEFUL FOR TODAY

"Dreams are necessary to life." - Anais Nin

never ever give up

Date: /   /

_____
_____
_____
_____
_____
_____
_____
_____
_____
_____
_____
_____
_____
_____
_____
_____
_____
_____

THINGS TO BE GRATEFUL FOR TODAY

> *"Dreams make things happen, nothing is impossible as long as you believe."* - Anonymous

Date: /   /   Take Action!

_____

_____

_____

_____

_____

_____

_____

_____

_____

_____

_____

_____

_____

_____

_____

_____

_____

THINGS TO BE GRATEFUL FOR TODAY

> *"Dream big dreams, commit to you true passion, and you will learn to fly."* - Vadim Kotelnikov

never ever give up

Date: /   /
_____
_____
_____
_____
_____
_____
_____
_____
_____
_____
_____
_____
_____
_____
_____
_____
_____
_____
_____
_____

THINGS TO BE GRATEFUL FOR TODAY

Date: /   /

think
positive

THINGS TO BE GRATEFUL FOR TODAY

"The only thing that stands between you and your dream is the will to try and the belief that it is actually possible." - Joel Brown

Date: /   /

never
ever
give
up

THINGS TO BE GRATEFUL FOR TODAY

Date: /   /   Take Action!

_____
_____
_____
_____
_____
_____
_____
_____
_____
_____
_____
_____
_____
_____
_____
_____
_____
_____

THINGS TO BE GRATEFUL FOR TODAY

"A champion is defined not by their wins but by how they can recover when they fall." - Serena Williams

never ever give up

Date: /   /

THINGS TO BE GRATEFUL FOR TODAY

Date: /   /

think positive

THINGS TO BE GRATEFUL FOR TODAY

"Dreams are extremely important. You can't do it unless you imagine it." - George Lucas

never ever give up

Date: /   /

_____

_____

_____

_____

_____

_____

_____

_____

_____

_____

_____

_____

_____

_____

_____

_____

_____

_____

THINGS TO BE GRATEFUL FOR TODAY

Date: /   /   Take Action!

THINGS TO BE GRATEFUL FOR TODAY

> *"Doing what you believe in, and going after your dreams will only result in success."* - Anonymous

never ever give up

Date: /   /

_____
_____
_____
_____
_____
_____
_____
_____
_____
_____
_____
_____
_____
_____
_____
_____
_____
_____
_____
_____

THINGS TO BE GRATEFUL FOR TODAY

Date: / /

think positive

THINGS TO BE GRATEFUL FOR TODAY

Date: /   /

never ever give up

THINGS TO BE GRATEFUL FOR TODAY

> *"Miracles start to happen when you give as much energy to your dreams as you do to your fears."* - Richard Wilkins

Date: /   /   *Take Action!*

_____
_____
_____
_____
_____
_____
_____
_____
_____
_____
_____
_____
_____
_____
_____
_____
_____

THINGS TO BE GRATEFUL FOR TODAY

"Let your dreams be bigger than your fears and your actions louder than your words." - Anonymous

never ever give up

Date: /   /

_____

_____

_____

_____

_____

_____

_____

_____

_____

_____

_____

_____

_____

_____

_____

_____

_____

_____

THINGS TO BE GRATEFUL FOR TODAY

"Life is like riding a bicycle. To keep your balance, you must keep moving." - Albert Einstein

think positive

Date: /   /

_____

_____

_____

_____

_____

_____

_____

_____

_____

_____

_____

_____

_____

_____

_____

_____

_____

THINGS TO BE GRATEFUL FOR TODAY

"It isn't where you came from. It's where you're going that counts." - Ella Fitzgerald

never
ever
give
up

Date: /   /

_____
_____
_____
_____
_____
_____
_____
_____
_____
_____
_____
_____
_____
_____
_____
_____
_____
_____
_____
_____
_____

THINGS TO BE GRATEFUL FOR TODAY

Date: /   /   Take Action!

_____

_____

_____

_____

_____

_____

_____

_____

_____

_____

_____

_____

_____

_____

_____

_____

_____

_____

_____

THINGS TO BE GRATEFUL FOR TODAY

"You are never too old to set another goal or to dream a new dream." - C.S Lewis

never ever give up

Date: /   /

_____

_____

_____

_____

_____

_____

_____

_____

_____

_____

_____

_____

_____

_____

_____

_____

_____

_____

THINGS TO BE GRATEFUL FOR TODAY

think positive

Date: /   /

_____

_____

_____

_____

_____

_____

_____

_____

_____

_____

_____

_____

_____

_____

_____

_____

_____

_____

_____

THINGS TO BE GRATEFUL FOR TODAY

"In the middle of every difficulty lies opportunity." –
Albert Einstein

never
ever
give
up

Date: /   /
_____
_____
_____
_____
_____
_____
_____
_____
_____
_____
_____
_____
_____
_____
_____
_____
_____
_____
_____

THINGS TO BE GRATEFUL FOR TODAY

Date: /   /

Take Action!

THINGS TO BE GRATEFUL FOR TODAY

"He who has a why to live can bear almost any how." –
Friedrich Nietzsche

never ever give up

Date: /   /

THINGS TO BE GRATEFUL FOR TODAY

think positive

Date: /   /

_____
_____
_____
_____
_____
_____
_____
_____
_____
_____
_____
_____
_____
_____
_____
_____
_____
_____

THINGS TO BE GRATEFUL FOR TODAY

"Don't let go of your dreams. If you have determination and belief in your dreams, you will succeed in spite of your desire to let go." - Catherine Pulsifer

make it happen

Date: __ / __ / __

THINGS TO BE GRATEFUL FOR TODAY

> *"Whatever you can do, or dream you can, begin it.*
> *Boldness has genius, power, and magic in it."* – Goethe

Date: /   /

Take Action!

_____

_____

_____

_____

_____

_____

_____

_____

_____

_____

_____

_____

_____

_____

_____

_____

_____

THINGS TO BE GRATEFUL FOR TODAY

"Have faith in yourself and in the future." – Ted Kennedy

think positive

Date: /   /

THINGS TO BE GRATEFUL FOR TODAY

Date: /   /

think positive

THINGS TO BE GRATEFUL FOR TODAY

"The most effective way to do it, is to do it."
— Amelia Earhart.

Take Action!

Date: /   /

_____

_____

_____

_____

_____

_____

_____

_____

_____

_____

_____

_____

_____

_____

_____

_____

_____

_____

THINGS TO BE GRATEFUL FOR TODAY

"If you take responsibility for yourself you will develop a hunger to accomplish your dreams." – Les Brown

think
positive

Date: /   /

_____
_____
_____
_____
_____
_____
_____
_____
_____
_____
_____
_____
_____
_____
_____
_____
_____
_____
_____
_____
_____

THINGS TO BE GRATEFUL FOR TODAY

"Forget about the fast lane. If you really want to fly, just harness your power to your passion." - Oprah.

make it happen

Date: /   /

THINGS TO BE GRATEFUL FOR TODAY

*"You can live your dreams if you can embrace change.
It's by taking chances that you'll learn how to be brave."*
— Nikita Koloff

Date: /   /

*think
positive*

THINGS TO BE GRATEFUL FOR TODAY

> *"If I can dream, I can act. And if I can act, I can become."* — Poh Yu Khing

make it happen

Date: /   /

THINGS TO BE GRATEFUL FOR TODAY

"Success happens when you are stronger than your excuses" — Frank Mullani

Date: /   /

think positive

THINGS TO BE GRATEFUL FOR TODAY

"The future belongs to those who believe in the beauty of their dreams." – Eleanor Roosevelt.

make it happen

Date: /   /

THINGS TO BE GRATEFUL FOR TODAY

Date: /   /

think positive

THINGS TO BE GRATEFUL FOR TODAY

"The secret of getting ahead is getting started."
— Sally Berger.

make it happen

Date: /   /

_____

THINGS TO BE GRATEFUL FOR TODAY

> *"Never give up on what you really want to do. The person with big dreams is more powerful than one with all the facts."* — Life's Little Instructions

think positive

Date: / /

THINGS TO BE GRATEFUL FOR TODAY

"Have the courage to follow your dreams. It's the first step towards attaining your destiny." – Nikita Koloff

make it happen

Date: /   /

_____

_____

_____

_____

_____

_____

_____

_____

_____

_____

_____

_____

_____

_____

_____

_____

_____

_____

_____

_____

THINGS TO BE GRATEFUL FOR TODAY

think positive

Date: /   /

_____

_____

_____

_____

_____

_____

_____

_____

_____

_____

_____

_____

_____

_____

_____

_____

THINGS TO BE GRATEFUL FOR TODAY

"It's better to have an impossible dream than no dream at all." – Anonymous

make it happen

Date: /   /
_____
_____
_____
_____
_____
_____
_____
_____
_____
_____
_____
_____
_____
_____
_____
_____
_____
_____
_____
_____

THINGS TO BE GRATEFUL FOR TODAY

Date: /   /

think positive

THINGS TO BE GRATEFUL FOR TODAY

"The question isn't who's going to let me; it's who is going to stop me." – Ayn Rand.

make
it
happen

Date: /   /

THINGS TO BE GRATEFUL FOR TODAY

> *"This one step: choosing a goal and sticking to it, changes everything."* – Scott Reed

Date: /   /

think positive

THINGS TO BE GRATEFUL FOR TODAY

"Always go with the choice that scares you the most, because that's the one that is going to require the most from you" – Caroline Myss.

make it happen

Date: /   /

THINGS TO BE GRATEFUL FOR TODAY

"Do you really want to look back on your life and see how wonderful it could have been had you not been afraid to live it?" – Caroline Myss.

think positive

Date: /   /

_____

_____

_____

_____

_____

_____

_____

_____

_____

_____

_____

_____

_____

_____

_____

_____

THINGS TO BE GRATEFUL FOR TODAY

"The most common way people give up their power is by thinking they don't have any." – Alice Walker.

never
ever
give
up

Date: /   /

THINGS TO BE GRATEFUL FOR TODAY

"At first, dreams seem impossible, then improbable, and eventually inevitable." – Christopher Reeve

think positive

Date: /   /

THINGS TO BE GRATEFUL FOR TODAY

Date: /   /

never ever give up

THINGS TO BE GRATEFUL FOR TODAY

think positive

Date: /   /

THINGS TO BE GRATEFUL FOR TODAY

> *"And the trouble is, if you don't risk anything, you risk more."* – Erica Jong.

Date: /   /

never ever give up

THINGS TO BE GRATEFUL FOR TODAY

think positive

Date: /   /

_____

_____

_____

_____

_____

_____

_____

_____

_____

_____

_____

_____

_____

_____

_____

_____

THINGS TO BE GRATEFUL FOR TODAY

Date: /   /

never ever give up

THINGS TO BE GRATEFUL FOR TODAY

Date: /   /

think positive

THINGS TO BE GRATEFUL FOR TODAY

> *"For those who dare to dream, there is a whole world to win."* — Dhirubhai Ambani

never ever give up

Date: /   /

_____

_____

_____

_____

_____

_____

_____

_____

_____

_____

_____

_____

_____

_____

_____

_____

_____

THINGS TO BE GRATEFUL FOR TODAY

"To accomplish great things, we must not only act but also dream; not only plan but also believe."
– Anatole France

think
positive

Date: ___ / ___ / ___

_____

_____

_____

_____

_____

_____

_____

_____

_____

_____

_____

_____

_____

_____

_____

_____

THINGS TO BE GRATEFUL FOR TODAY

> *"I'm not afraid of storms, for I'm learning to sail my ship."* – Louisa May Alcott.

never ever give up

Date: /   /

_____
_____
_____
_____
_____
_____
_____
_____
_____
_____
_____
_____
_____
_____
_____
_____
_____

THINGS TO BE GRATEFUL FOR TODAY

Date: /   /

think positive

THINGS TO BE GRATEFUL FOR TODAY

> *"When you have a dream you've got to grab it and never let go."* – Carol Burnett

never ever give up

Date: /   /

_____
_____
_____
_____
_____
_____
_____
_____
_____
_____
_____
_____
_____
_____
_____
_____
_____
_____
_____
_____

THINGS TO BE GRATEFUL FOR TODAY

"Follow your heart and your dreams will come true."
— Anonymous

Date: /   /   Take Action!

_____
_____
_____
_____
_____
_____
_____
_____
_____
_____
_____
_____
_____
_____
_____
_____
_____
_____

THINGS TO BE GRATEFUL FOR TODAY

"Go confidently in the direction of your dreams. Live the life you've imagined." – Henry David Thoreau

Date: /   /

think
positive

_____
_____
_____
_____
_____
_____
_____
_____
_____
_____
_____
_____
_____
_____
_____
_____
_____

THINGS TO BE GRATEFUL FOR TODAY

Date: /   /   *Take Action!*

_____

_____

_____

_____

_____

_____

_____

_____

_____

_____

_____

_____

_____

_____

_____

_____

_____

THINGS TO BE GRATEFUL FOR TODAY

"Difficult roads often lead to beautiful destinations"

Date: /   /

think positive

THINGS TO BE GRATEFUL FOR TODAY

Date: /   /   Take Action!

_____

_____

_____

_____

_____

_____

_____

_____

_____

_____

_____

_____

_____

_____

_____

_____

_____

THINGS TO BE GRATEFUL FOR TODAY

Date: /   /

think positive

THINGS TO BE GRATEFUL FOR TODAY

Take Action!

Date: /   /

_____

_____

_____

_____

_____

_____

_____

_____

_____

_____

_____

_____

_____

_____

THINGS TO BE GRATEFUL FOR TODAY

"Dreams are the touchstones of our character."
— Henry David Thoreau

think
positive

Date: /   /
_____
_____
_____
_____
_____
_____
_____
_____
_____
_____
_____
_____
_____
_____
_____
_____
_____
_____

THINGS TO BE GRATEFUL FOR TODAY

Take Action!

Date: /   /

_____

_____

_____

_____

_____

_____

_____

_____

_____

_____

_____

_____

_____

_____

_____

_____

_____

_____

_____

THINGS TO BE GRATEFUL FOR TODAY

"Believe you can and you are halfway there"
– T. Roosevelt

think
positive

Date: /   /

_____

_____

_____

_____

_____

_____

_____

_____

_____

_____

_____

_____

_____

_____

_____

_____

_____

THINGS TO BE GRATEFUL FOR TODAY

Date: /   /

Take Action!

THINGS TO BE GRATEFUL FOR TODAY

"You are capable of amazing things"

Date: /   /

think
positive

THINGS TO BE GRATEFUL FOR TODAY

Date: /   /   Take Action!

THINGS TO BE GRATEFUL FOR TODAY

> *"If you really want to do it, you do it. There are no excuses."* — Bruce Nauman

think positive

Date: /   /

_____
_____
_____
_____
_____
_____
_____
_____
_____
_____
_____
_____
_____
_____
_____
_____
_____
_____

THINGS TO BE GRATEFUL FOR TODAY

"Nothing will work unless you do" – Maya Angelou

Date: /   /

Take Action!

_____
_____
_____
_____
_____
_____
_____
_____
_____
_____
_____
_____
_____
_____
_____
_____
_____
_____

THINGS TO BE GRATEFUL FOR TODAY

"Always remember, you have within you the strength, the patience, and the passion to reach for the stars to change the world." — Harriet Tubman

think positive

Date: /   /

_____

_____

_____

_____

_____

_____

_____

_____

_____

_____

_____

_____

_____

_____

_____

_____

_____

THINGS TO BE GRATEFUL FOR TODAY

"Make it Happen"

Take Action!

Date: /   /

_____
_____
_____
_____
_____
_____
_____
_____
_____
_____
_____
_____
_____
_____
_____
_____
_____
_____

THINGS TO BE GRATEFUL FOR TODAY

Date: /   /

think positive

THINGS TO BE GRATEFUL FOR TODAY

"Ninety-nine percent of the failures come from people who have the habit of making excuses."
— George Washington Carver

Date: /   /

Take Action!

_____

_____

_____

_____

_____

_____

_____

_____

_____

_____

_____

_____

_____

_____

_____

_____

THINGS TO BE GRATEFUL FOR TODAY

"The secret of getting ahead is getting started."
— Sally Berger

think
positive

Date: /   /

THINGS TO BE GRATEFUL FOR TODAY

Date: /   /

Take Action!

THINGS TO BE GRATEFUL FOR TODAY

"A man can fail many times, but he isn't a failure until he begins to blame somebody else." — *John Burroughs*

Date: /   /

think positive

THINGS TO BE GRATEFUL FOR TODAY

Date: /   /   Take Action!

THINGS TO BE GRATEFUL FOR TODAY